Theod

& Facts

By Blago Kirov

First Edition

Translated by Raia Iotova

*****

Theodore Roosevelt: Quotes & Facts
*****

MW01115432

Copyright © 2016 by Blago Kirov

Foreword

"Speak softly and carry a big stick; you will go far."

This book is an anthology of quotes from Theodore Roosevelt and selected facts about Theodore Roosevelt.

"The worst of all fears is the fear of living"

"Whenever you are asked if you can do a job, tell 'am, 'Certainly I can!' Then get busy and find out how to do it."

"Americanism is a question of principle, of idealism, of character. It is not a matter of birthplace, or creed, or line of descent."

"If you've got them by the balls, their hearts and minds will follow."

"In any moment of decision, the best thing you can do is the right thing, the next best thing is the wrong thing, and the worst thing you can do is nothing."

"The government is us; WE are the government, you and I."

"Do what you can, where you are, with what you have."

"90% of the work in this country is done by people who don't feel good"."

"A great democracy has got to be progressive or it will soon cease to be great or a democracy."

Theodore was the second of four children born to socialite Martha Stewart "Mittie" Bulloch and glass businessman and philanthropist Theodore Roosevelt, Sr.

His brother Elliott was the father of First Lady Anna Eleanor Roosevelt, the wife of President Franklin Delano Roosevelt.

His paternal grandfather was of Dutch descent; his other ancestry included English, Scots-Irish, Scottish, Welsh, French, and German.

His father had been a prominent leader in New York's cultural affairs; he helped to found the Metropolitan Museum of Art, and had been especially active in mobilizing support for the Union war effort.

Before he entered Harvard College on September 27, 1876, his father told him "Take care of your morals first, your health next, and finally your studies".

After Harvard Roosevelt entered Columbia Law School, and was an able student, but he often found law to be irrational; he spent much of his time writing a book on the War of 1812.

In 1905, Roosevelt offered to mediate a treaty to end the Russo-Japanese War. Roosevelt won the Nobel Peace Prize for his successful efforts.

Roosevelt was an avid reader of poetry. Poet Robert Frost said that Roosevelt "was our kind. He quoted poetry to me. He knew poetry."

In all, Roosevelt wrote about 18 books (each in several editions), including his autobiography, The Rough Riders, History of the Naval War of 1812, and others on subjects such as ranching, explorations, and wildlife. His most ambitious book was the four volume narrative The Winning of the West, focused on the American frontier in the 18th and early 19th centuries.

Roosevelt was an avid reader, reading tens of thousands of books, at a rate of several per day in multiple languages.

Along with Thomas Jefferson, Roosevelt was the most well-read of all American politicians.

Roosevelt was included with Presidents George Washington, Thomas Jefferson, and Abraham Lincoln at the Mount Rushmore Memorial, designed in 1927 with the approval of Republican President Calvin Coolidge

President Bill Clinton awarded Theodore Roosevelt the Medal of Honor posthumously for his charge on San Juan Hill, Cuba, during the Spanish–American War.

Some Facts about Theodore Roosevelt

Theodore Roosevelt was born on October 27, 1858, in a four-story brownstone at 28 East 20th Street, in Manhattan, New York.

Theodore was the second of four children born to socialite Martha Stewart "Mittie" Bulloch and glass businessman and philanthropist Theodore Roosevelt, Sr.

He had an older sister, Anna (nicknamed "Bamie"), a younger brother, Elliott, and a younger sister, Corinne.

His brother Elliott was the father of First Lady Anna Eleanor Roosevelt, the wife of President Franklin Delano Roosevelt.

His paternal grandfather was of Dutch descent; his other ancestry included English, Scots-Irish, Scottish, Welsh, French, and German.

Roosevelt's youth was largely shaped by his poor health and debilitating asthma.

His lifelong interest in zoology began at age seven. At age nine, he recorded his observation of insects in a paper entitled "The Natural History of Insects".

His father had been a prominent leader in New York's cultural affairs; he helped to found the Metropolitan Museum of Art, and had been especially active in mobilizing support for the Union war effort.

After being manhandled by two older boys on a camping trip, he found a boxing coach to teach him to fight.

Roosevelt was mostly home schooled by tutors and his parents. He was solid in geography (as a result of self study during travels with parents), and bright in history, biology, French, and German; but he struggled in mathematics and the classical languages.

Before he entered Harvard College on September 27, 1876, his father told him "Take care of your morals first, your health next, and finally your studies".

While at Harvard he did well in science, philosophy, and rhetoric courses but continued to struggle in Latin and Greek. He studied biology intently and was already an accomplished naturalist and a published ornithologist.

Roosevelt participated in rowing and boxing; he was once runner-up in a Harvard boxing tournament.

Roosevelt was a member of the Alpha Delta Phi literary society, the Delta Kappa Epsilon fraternity, and the Porcellian Club he was also an editor of The Harvard Advocate.

Roosevelt read prodigiously with an almost photographic memory.

On June 30, 1880, Roosevelt graduated Phi Beta Kappa (22nd of 177) from Harvard with an A.B. magna cum laude.

After Harvard Roosevelt entered Columbia Law School, and was an able student, but he often found law to be irrational; he spent much of his time writing a book on the War of 1812.

On his 22nd birthday, Roosevelt married socialite Alice Hathaway Lee, daughter of banker George Cabot Lee and Caroline Watts Haskell. Their daughter, Alice Lee Roosevelt, was born on February 12, 1884.

Roosevelt's wife died two days after giving birth due to an undiagnosed case of kidney failure (called Bright's disease at the time), which had been masked by the pregnancy. In his diary, Roosevelt wrote a large 'X' on the page and then, "The light has gone out of my life." His mother, Mittie, had died of typhoid fever eleven hours earlier at 3:00 a.m., in the same house. Distraught, Roosevelt left baby Alice in the care of his sister Bamie in New York City while he grieved. He assumed custody of his daughter when she was three. For the rest of his life, he rarely spoke about his wife Alice and did not write about her in his autobiography.

Roosevelt was a member of the New York State Assembly (New York Co., 21st D.) in 1882, 1883 and 1884. In 1883, he became the Assembly Minority Leader.

In 1886, Roosevelt was the Republican candidate for mayor of New York City, portraying himself as "The Cowboy of the Dakotas"; he took third place with 27%.

Roosevelt built a ranch named Elk Horn, thirty-five miles (56 km) north of the boomtown of Medora, North Dakota. On the banks of the Little Missouri, Roosevelt learned to ride western style, rope and hunt.

As a deputy sheriff, Roosevelt pursued three outlaws who had stolen his riverboat and escaped north up the Little Missouri. He captured them, but decided against a vigilante hanging; instead, he sent his foreman back by boat, and conveyed the thieves to Dickinson for trial. He assumed guard over them for forty hours without sleep, while reading Leo Tolstoy to keep himself awake. On another occasion, while searching for a group of relentless horse thieves, Roosevelt met Seth Bullock, the famous sheriff of Deadwood, South Dakota. The two would remain friends for life.

On December 2, 1886, Roosevelt married his childhood and family friend, Edith Kermit Carow (August 6, 1861 – September 30, 1948), a daughter of Charles Carow and Gertrude Elizabeth Tyler. They had five children: Theodore "Ted" III (1887–1944), Kermit (1889–1943), Ethel (1891–1977), Archibald (1894–1979), and Quentin (1897–1918).

In the 1888 presidential election, Roosevelt successfully campaigned, primarily in the Midwest, for Benjamin Harrison. President Harrison appointed Roosevelt to the United States Civil Service Commission, where he served until 1895.

In 1894, a group of reform Republicans approached Roosevelt about running for Mayor of New York again; he declined, mostly due to his wife's resistance to being removed from the Washington social set.

Roosevelt became president of the board of the New York City Police Commissioners for two years in 1895 and radically reformed the police force. The New York Police Department (NYPD) was reputed as one of the most corrupt in America; the NYPD's history division records that Roosevelt was "an iron-willed leader of unimpeachable honesty, (who) brought a reforming zeal to the New York City Police Commission in 1895."

Roosevelt had demonstrated, through his research and writing, a fascination with naval history; President William McKinley, urged by Roosevelt's close friend Congressman Henry Cabot Lodge, appointed Roosevelt as the Assistant Secretary of the Navy in 1897. Ten days after the battleship Maine exploded in the harbor of Havana, Cuba, the Secretary left the office and Roosevelt became Acting Secretary for four hours. Roosevelt cabled the Navy worldwide to prepare for war, ordered ammunition and supplies, brought in experts and went to Congress asking for the authority to recruit as many sailors as he wanted. Roosevelt was instrumental in preparing the Navy for the Spanish–American War.

Prior to his service in the Spanish–American War, Roosevelt had already seen reserve military service from 1882 to 1886 with the New York National Guard. Commissioned on August 1, 1882 as a 2nd Lieutenant with B Company, 8th Regiment, he was promoted to Captain and company commander a year later.

When the United States and Spain declared war against each other in late April 1898, Roosevelt resigned from his civilian leadership job with the Navy on May 6 and formed the First US Volunteer Cavalry Regiment along with Army Colonel Leonard Wood. Under his leadership, the Rough Riders became famous for the charge up Kettle Hill on July 1, 1898, while supporting the regulars. Roosevelt always recalled the Battle of Kettle Hill (part of the San Juan Heights) as "the great day of my life" and "my crowded hour".

After leaving the Army, Roosevelt discovered that New York Republicans needed him, because their current governor was tainted by scandal and would probably lose. He campaigned vigorously on his war record, winning the 1898 state election by a historical margin of 1%. As governor, Roosevelt learned much about ongoing economic issues and political techniques that later proved valuable in his presidency.

In November 1899, William McKinley's first Vice-President Garret Hobart died of heart failure. Theodore Roosevelt had anticipated a second term as governor or, alternatively, a cabinet post in the War Department; McKinley refused to consider Roosevelt as Secretary of War, but saw no risk in making him Vice President. Roosevelt accepted the nomination, although his campaign manager, Mark Hanna, thought Roosevelt was too cowboy-like. Roosevelt's six months as Vice President (March to September 1901) were uneventful with one singular exception: On September 2, 1901, Roosevelt first publicized an aphorism that thrilled his supporters at the Minnesota State Fair: "Speak softly and carry a big stick, and you will go far."

On September 6, 1901, President McKinley was shot by an anarchist acting alone while in Buffalo, New York. McKinley died on September 14, and Roosevelt was sworn in at the Ansley Wilcox House. Roosevelt kept McKinley's Cabinet and promised to continue McKinley's policies.

Roosevelt kept McKinley's Cabinet and promised to continue McKinley's policies.

For his aggressive use of United States antitrust law, Roosevelt became known as the "trust-buster". He brought 40 antitrust suits, and broke up major companies, such as the largest railroad and Standard Oil, the largest oil company.

Roosevelt served as honorary president of the American School Hygiene Association from 1907 to 1908, and in 1909 he convened the first White House Conference on the Care of Dependent Children.

Roosevelt's willingness to exercise his power included attempted rule changes in the game of football; at the Naval Academy, he sought to force retention of martial arts classes and to revise disciplinary rules. He even ordered changes made in the minting of a coin whose design he disliked, and ordered the Government Printing Office to adopt simplified spellings for a core list of 300 words, according to reformers on the Simplified Spelling Board.

Roosevelt established the United States Forest Service, signed into law the creation of five National Parks, and signed the 1906 Antiquities Act, under which he proclaimed 18 new U.S. National Monuments.

Roosevelt established the first 51 Bird Reserves, four Game Preserves, and 150 National Forests, including Shoshone National Forest, the nation's first. The area of the United States that he placed under public protection totals approximately 230,000,000 acres (930,000 km2).

As president, Roosevelt primarily focused the nation's overseas ambitions on the Caribbean, especially locations that had a bearing on the defense of his pet project, the Panama Canal.

In 1905, Roosevelt offered to mediate a treaty to end the Russo-Japanese War. Roosevelt won the Nobel Peace Prize for his successful efforts.

Building on McKinley's effective use of the press, Roosevelt made the White House the center of news every day, providing interviews and photo opportunities. After noticing the reporters huddled outside the White House in the rain one day, he gave them their own room inside, effectively inventing the presidential press briefing. The grateful press, with unprecedented access to the White House, rewarded Roosevelt with ample coverage.

Roosevelt loved talking with intellectuals, authors, and writers.

The Democratic Party's nominee in 1904 was Alton Brooks Parker. Roosevelt won 56% of the popular vote, and Parker received 38%; Roosevelt also won the Electoral College vote, 336 to 140. Before his inauguration ceremony, Roosevelt declared that he would not serve another term.

Before leaving office, while attempting to push through the nomination of William Howard Taft for the Presidency in 1908, Roosevelt declared Taft to be a "genuine progressive".

In March 1909, shortly after the end of his presidency, Roosevelt left New York for the Smithsonian-Roosevelt African Expedition, a safari in east and central Africa outfitted by the Smithsonian Institution. Roosevelt and his companions killed or trapped approximately 11,400 animals, from insects and moles to hippopotamuses and elephants. The 1000 large animals included 512 big game animals, including six rare White rhinos. Tons of salted animals and their skins were shipped to Washington; it took years to mount them all, and the Smithsonian shared many duplicate specimens with other museums.

Roosevelt became a life member of the National Rifle Association in 1907.

When World War I began in 1914, Roosevelt strongly supported the Allies and demanded a harsher policy against Germany, especially regarding submarine warfare. Roosevelt angrily denounced the foreign policy of President Wilson, calling it a failure regarding the atrocities in Belgium and the violations of American rights.

In November 1911, a group of Ohio Republicans endorsed Roosevelt for the party's nomination for president; the endorsers included James R. Garfield and Dan Hanna. The 1912 primaries represented the first extensive use of the presidential primary, a reform achievement of the progressive movement. Roosevelt won in Illinois, Minnesota, Nebraska, South Dakota, California, Maryland and Pennsylvania; Roosevelt also won Taft's home state of Ohio. These primary elections, while demonstrating Roosevelt's continuing popularity with the electorate, were not pivotal. The final credentials of the state delegates at the national convention were determined by the national committee, which was controlled by the party leaders, headed by the incumbent president. At the Republican Convention in Chicago, though Taft's victory was not immediate, the ultimate outcome was inevitably in his favor.

On October 14, 1912, while campaigning in Milwaukee, Wisconsin, Roosevelt was shot by a saloonkeeper named John Flammang Schrank. The bullet lodged in his chest after penetrating his steel eyeglass case and passing through a thick (50 pages) single-folded copy of the speech he was carrying in his jacket. Roosevelt, as an experienced hunter and anatomist, correctly concluded that since he was not coughing blood, the bullet had not reached his lung, and he declined suggestions to go to the hospital immediately. Instead, he delivered his scheduled speech with blood seeping into his shirt. He spoke for 90 minutes. Roosevelt carried the bullet with him for the rest of his life.

A friend of Roosevelt's, Father John Augustine Zahm, a Catholic priest and scientist at the University of Notre Dame, had searched for new adventures and found them in the forests of South America. After a briefing of several of his own expeditions, he persuaded Roosevelt to participate in such an expedition in 1912. To finance the expedition, Roosevelt received support from the American Museum of Natural History, promising to bring back many new animal specimens. Roosevelt's popular book, Through the Brazilian Wilderness describes his expedition into the Brazilian jungle in 1913 as a member of the Roosevelt-Rondon Scientific Expedition, co-named after its leader, Brazilian explorer Cândido Rondon. The book describes the scientific discovery, scenic tropical vistas, and exotic flora and fauna experienced during the adventure.

On the night of January 5, 1919, Roosevelt experienced breathing problems. He felt better after treatment from his physician, Dr. George W. Faller, and went to bed. Roosevelt's last words were "Please put out that light, James" to his family servant James Amos. Between 4:00 AM and 4:15 AM the next morning, Roosevelt died in his sleep at Sagamore Hill as a result of a blood clot detaching from a vein and traveling to his lungs.

Upon receiving word of his death, his son Archibald telegraphed his siblings simply, "The old lion is dead.

Roosevelt was an avid reader of poetry. Poet Robert Frost said that Roosevelt "was our kind. He quoted poetry to me. He knew poetry."

In all, Roosevelt wrote about 18 books (each in several editions), including his autobiography, The Rough Riders, History of the Naval War of 1812, and others on subjects such as ranching, explorations, and wildlife. His most ambitious book was the four volume narrative The Winning of the West, focused on the American frontier in the 18th and early 19th centuries.

Roosevelt was an avid reader, reading tens of thousands of books, at a rate of several per day in multiple languages.

Along with Thomas Jefferson, Roosevelt was the most well-read of all American politicians.

Roosevelt was included with Presidents George Washington, Thomas Jefferson, and Abraham Lincoln at the Mount Rushmore Memorial, designed in 1927 with the approval of Republican President Calvin Coolidge

President Bill Clinton awarded Theodore Roosevelt the Medal of Honor posthumously for his charge on San Juan Hill, Cuba, during the Spanish–American War.

The United States Navy named two ships for Roosevelt: the USS Theodore Roosevelt, a submarine that was in commission from 1961 to 1982, and the USS Theodore Roosevelt, an aircraft carrier that has been on active duty in the Atlantic Fleet since 1986.

Theodore Roosevelt was one of the first presidents whose voice was recorded for posterity. Several of his recorded speeches survive.

One lasting, popular legacy of Roosevelt is the stuffed toy bears — teddy bears — named after him following an incident on a hunting trip in Mississippi in 1902. Roosevelt famously refused to shoot a defenseless black bear that had been tied to a tree. After the cartoonist Clifford K. Berryman illustrated the President with a bear, a toy maker heard the story and named the teddy bear after Roosevelt. Bears, and later bear cubs, became closely associated with Roosevelt in political cartoons, despite Roosevelt openly despising being called "Teddy".

His Words

"Speak softly and carry a big stick; you will go far."

"The worst of all fears is the fear of living"

"Whenever you are asked if you can do a job, tell 'am, 'Certainly I can!' Then get busy and find out how to do it."

"Americanism is a question of principle, of idealism, of character. It is not a matter of birthplace, or creed, or line of descent."

"If you've got them by the balls, their hearts and minds will follow."

"In any moment of decision, the best thing you can do is the right thing, the next best thing is the wrong thing, and the worst thing you can do is nothing."

"The government is us; WE are the government, you and I."

"Do what you can, where you are, with what you have."

"90% of the work in this country is done by people who don't feel good"."

"A great democracy has got to be progressive or it will soon cease to be great or a democracy."

"A man who has never gone to school may steal from a freight car; but if he has a university education he may steal the whole railroad."

"A thorough knowledge of the Bible is worth more than a college education."

"A vote is like a rifle: its usefulness depends upon the character of the user."

"Aggressive fighting for the right is the noblest sport the world affords."

"All the resources we need are in the mind."

"Although not a very old man, I have yet lived a great deal in my life, and I have known sorrow too bitter and joy too keen to allow me to become either cast down or elated for more than a very brief period over any success or defeat."

"And it is through strife and the readiness for strife that a man or a nation must win greatness. So, let the world know that we are here and willing to pour out our blood, our treasure, our tears. And that America is ready and if need be desirous of battle"

"Any man who tries to excite class hatred, sectional hate, hate of creeds, any kind of hatred in our community, though he may affect to do it in the interest of the class he is addressing, is in the long run with absolute certainly that class's own worst enemy."

"At times a man must cut loose from his associates and stand alone for a great cause; but the necessity for such action is almost as rare as the necessity for revolution."

"Be practical as well as generous in your ideals. Keep your eyes on the stars, but remember to keep your feet on the ground."

"Behind the ostensible government sits enthroned an invisible government owing no allegiance and acknowledging no responsibility to the people. To destroy this invisible government, to befoul the unholy alliance between corrupt business and corrupt politics is the first task of the statesmanship of today."

"Believe you can and you're half way there."

"Bodily vigor is good, and vigor of intellect is even better, but far above both is character. It is true, of course, that a genius may, on certain lines, do more than a brave and manly fellow who is not a genius; and so, in sports, vast physical strength may overcome weakness, even though the puny body may have in it the heart of a lion. But, in the long run, in the great battle of life, no brilliancy of intellect, no perfection of bodily development, will count when weighed in the balance against that assemblage of virtues, active and passive, of moral qualities, which we group together under the name of character; and if between any two contestants, even in college sport or in college work, the difference in character on the right side is as great as the difference of intellect or strength the other way, it is the character side that will win."

"Character, in the long run, is the decisive factor in the life of an individual and of nations alike."

"Comparison is the thief of joy."

"Courage is not having the strength to go on; it is going on when you don't have the strength."

"Courtesy is as much a mark of a gentleman as courage."

"Credit should go with the performance of duty, and not with what is very often the accident of glory."

"Don't hit at all if it is honorably possible to avoid hitting; but never hit soft!"

"Dreams are a dime a dozen. it's their execution that counts"

"Each one must do his part if we wish to show that the nation is worthy of its good fortune."

"Every immigrant who comes here should be required within five years to learn English or leave the country."

"Every reform movement has a lunatic fringe."

"Far and away the best prize that life has to offer is the chance to work hard at work worth doing."

"Far better it is to dare mighty things, to win glorious triumphs, even though checkered by failure, than to take rank with those poor spirits who neither enjoy much nor suffer much, because they live in the gray twilight that knows neither victory nor defeat."

"Fellow-feeling. . .is the most important factor in producing a healthy political and social life. Neither our national nor our local civic life can be what it should be unless it is marked by the fellow-feeling, the mutual kindness, the mutual respect, the sense of common duties and common interests, which arise when men take the trouble to understand one another, and to associate together for a common object. A very large share of the rancor of political and social strife arises either from sheer misunderstanding by one section, or by one class, of another, or else from the fact that the two sections, or two classes, are so cut off from each other that neither appreciates the other's passions, prejudices, and, indeed, point of view, while they are both entirely ignorant of their community of feeling as regards the essentials of manhood and humanity."

"For those who fight for it life has a flavor the sheltered will never know"

"For us is the life of action, of strenuous performance of duty; let us live in the harness, striving mightily; let us rather run the risk of wearing out than rusting out."

"Great corporations exist only because they are created and safeguarded by our institutions; and it is therefore our right and duty to see that they work in harmony with these institutions."

"Great thoughts speak only to the thoughtful mind, but great actions speak to all mankind."

"Hamilton, the most brilliant American statesman who ever lived, possessing the loftiest and keenest intellect of his time, was of course easily the foremost champion in the ranks of the New York Federalists; second to him came Jay, pure, strong and healthy in heart, body, and mind. Both of them watched with uneasy alarm the rapid drift toward anarchy; and both put forth all their efforts to stem the tide. They were of course too great men to fall in with the views of those whose antagonism to tyranny made them averse from order. They had little sympathy with the violent prejudices produced by the war. In particular they abhorred the vindictive laws directed against the persons and property of Tories; and they had the manliness to come forward as the defenders of the helpless and excessively unpopular Loyalists. They put a stop to the wrongs which were being inflicted on these men, and finally succeeded in having them restored to legal equality with other citizens, standing up with generous fearlessness against the clamor of the mob."

"Here is your country. Cherish these natural wonders, cherish the natural resources, cherish the history and romance as a sacred heritage, for your children and your children's children. Do not let selfish men or greedy interests skin your country of its beauty, its riches or its romance."

"I am a part of everything that I have read."

"I am an American; free born and free bred, where I acknowledge no man as my superior, except for his own worth, or as my inferior, except for his own demerit."

"I am a strong individualist by personal habit, inheritance, and conviction; but it is a mere matter of common sense to recognize that the State, the community, the citizens acting together, can do a number of things better than if they were left to individual action."

"I am no advocate of senseless and excessive cramming in studies, but a boy should work, and should work hard, at his lessons -- in the first place, for the sake of what he will learn, and in the next place, for the sake of the effect upon his own character of resolutely settling down to learn it. Shiftlessness, slackness, indifference in studying, are almost certain to mean inability to get on in other walks of life."

"I am only an average man, but by George, I work harder at it than the average man."

"I believe you can and you're already there"

"I care not what others think of what I do, but I care very much about what I think of what I do! That is character!"

"I f he fails, at least fails while daring greatly, so that his place shall never be with those cold and timid souls who neither know victory nor defeat."

"I had always felt that if there were a serious war I wished to be in a position to explain to my children why I did take part in it, and not why I did not take part in it."

"I have a perfect horror of words that are not backed up by deeds."

"I have never in my life envied a human being who led an easy life; I have envied a great many people who led difficult lives and led them well."

"I have only a second rate brain, but I think I have a capacity for action."

"I put myself in the way of things happening, and they happened."

"I stand for the square deal," Roosevelt said. "But when I say that I am for the square deal, I mean not merely that I stand for fair play under the present rules of the game, but that I stand for having those rules changed so as to work for a more substantial equality of opportunity and of reward for equally good service. One word of warning, which, I think, is hardly necessary in Kansas. When I say I want a square deal for the poor man, I do not mean that I want a square deal for the man who remains poor because he has not got the energy to work for himself. If a man who has had a chance will not make good, then he has got to quit."

"I wish to preach, not the doctrine of ignoble ease, but the doctrine of the strenuous life, the life of effort, labor and strife; to preach that highest form of success which comes, not the the man who desires mere easy peace, but to the man who does not shrink from danger, from hardship, or from bitter toil, and who out of these wins the splendid ultimate triumph."

"I would rather go out of politics having the feeling that I had done what was right than stay in with the approval of all men, knowing in my heart that I have acted as I ought not to."

"If a nation shows that it knows how to act with reasonable efficiency and decency in social and political matters, if it keeps order and pays its obligations, it need fear no interference from the United States."

"If given the choice between Righteousness and Peace, I choose Righteousness."

"If there is not the war, you don't get the great general; if there is not a great occasion, you don't get a great statesman; if Lincoln had lived in a time of peace, no one would have known his name."

"If there is one tendency of the day which more than any other is unhealthy and undesirable, it is the tendency to deify mere "smartness," unaccompanied by a sense of moral accountability. We shall never make our republic what it should be until as a people we thoroughly understand and put in practice the doctrine that success is abhorrent if attained by the sacrifice of the fundamental principles of morality."

"If you could kick the person in the pants responsible for most of your trouble, you wouldn't sit for a month."

"In advocating any measure we must consider not only its justice but its practicability."

"In foreign affairs we must make up our minds that, whether we wish it or not, we are a great people and must play a great part in the world. It is not open to us to choose whether we will play that great part or not. We have to play it. All we can decide is whether we shall play it well or ill."

"In life, as in football, the principle to follow is to hit the line hard."

"In order to succeed we need leaders of inspired idealism, leaders to whom are granted great visions, who dream greatly and strive to make their dreams come true; who can kindle the people with the fire from their own burning souls. The leader for the time being, whoever he may be, is but an instrument, to be used until broken and then to be cast aside; and if he is worth his salt he will care no more when he is broken than a soldier cares when he is sent where his life is forfeit in order that the victory may be won."

"In the first place, we should insist that if the immigrant who comes here in good faith becomes an American and assimilates himself to us, he shall be treated on an exact equality with everyone else, for it is an outrage to discriminate against any such man because of creed, or birthplace, or origin. But this is predicated upon the person's becoming in every facet an American, and nothing but an American...There can be no divided allegiance here. Any man who says he is an American, but something else also, isn't an American at all. We have room for but one flag, the American flag... We have room for but one language here, and that is the English language... and we have room for but one sole loyalty and that is a loyalty to the American people."

"In this country we have no place for hyphenated Americans."

"It behooves every man to remember that the work of the critic is of altogether secondary importance, and that in the end, progress is accomplished by the man who does things."

"It is a mere truism to say that every nation, whether in America or anywhere else, which desires to maintain its freedom, its independence, must ultimately realize that the right of such independence cannot be separated from the responsibility of making good use of it."

"It is better to have it and need it, than to need it and not have it."

"It is hard to fail, but it is worse never to have tried to succeed."

"It is no use to preach to children if you do not act decently yourself."

"It is not often that a man can make opportunities for himself. But he can put himself in such shape that when or if the opportunities come he is ready."

"It is not the critic who counts; not the man who points out how the strong man stumbles, or where the doer of deeds could have done them better. The credit belongs to the man who is actually in the arena, whose face is marred by dust and sweat and blood; who strives valiantly; who errs, who comes short again and again, because there is no effort without error and shortcoming; but who does actually strive to do the deeds; who knows great enthusiasms, the great devotions; who spends himself in a worthy cause; who at the best knows in the end the triumph of high achievement, and who at the worst, if he fails, at least fails while daring greatly, so that his place shall never be with those cold and timid souls who neither know victory nor defeat."

"It is out of the question for our people to rise by treading down any of their own number."

"It is true of the Nation, as of the individual, that the greatest doer must also be a great dreamer."

"It may be true that he travels farthest who travels alone, but the goal thus reached is not worth reaching."

"It tires me to talk to rich men. You expect a man of millions, the head of a great industry, to be a man worthhearing; but as a rule they don't know anything outside their own business."

"It was a pleasure to deal with a man of high ideals, who scorned everything mean and base, and who possessed those robust and hardy qualities of body and mind, for the lack of which no merely negative virtue can ever atone."

"Justice consists not in being neutral between right and wrong, but finding out the right and upholding it, wherever found, against the wrong."

"Keep your eyes on the stars, and your feet on the ground."

"Knowing what's right doesn't mean much unless you do what's right."

"Leave it as it is. The ages have been at work on it and man can only mar it."

"Let the watchwords of all our people be the old familiar watchwords of honesty, decency, fair-dealing, and commonsense."... "We must treat each man on his worth and merits as a man. We must see that each is given a square deal, because he is entitled to no more and should receive no less.""The welfare of each of us is dependent fundamentally upon the welfare of all of us."

"Life means change; where there is no change, death comes."

"Look Toward the stars but keep your feet firmly on the ground."

"More and more it is evident that the State, and if necessary the nation, has got to possess the right of supervision and control as regards the great corporations which are its creatures."

"Never throughout history has a man who lived a life of ease left a name worth remembering."

"Nine tenths of wisdom consists in being wise in time."

"No ability, no strength and force, no power of intellect or power of wealth, shall avail us, if we have not the root of right living in us."

"No man in public position can, under penalty of forfeiting the right to the respect of those whose regard he most values, fail as the opportunity comes to do all that in him lies for peace."

"No man is above the law, and no man is below it."

"No man is justified in doing evil on the ground of expediency."

"No man needs sympathy because he has to work, because he has a burden to carry. Far and away the best prize that life offers is the chance to work hard at work worth doing."

"No man should receive a dollar unless that dollar has been fairly earned."

"No one cares how much you know, until they know
how much you care"

"Nobody cares how much you know, until they know
how much you care."

"Nothing in the world is worth having or worth doing unless it means effort, pain, difficulty... I have never in my life envied a human being who led an easy life. I have envied a great many people who led difficult lives and led them well."

"Nothing worth having was ever achieved without effort"

"Of all the questions which can come before this nation, short of the actual preservation of its existence in a great war, there is none which compares in importance with the great central task of leaving this land even a better land for our descendants than it is for us."

"Only those are fit to live who do not fear to die; and none are fit to die who have shrunk from the joy of life and the duty of life. Both life and death are parts of the same Great Adventure."

"Order without liberty and liberty without order are equally destructive."

"Peace is normally a great good, and normally it coincides with righteousness, but it is righteousness and not peace which should bind the conscience of a nation as it should bind the conscience of an individual; and neither a nation nor an individual can surrender conscience to another's keeping."

"Our aim is not to do away with corporations; on the contrary, these big aggregations are an inevitable development of modern industrialism, and the effort to destroy them would be futile unless accomplished in ways that would work the utmost mischief to the entire body politic. We can do nothing of good in the way of regulating and supervising these corporations until we fix clearly in our minds that we are not attacking the corporations, but endeavoring to do away with any evil in them. We are not hostile to them; we are merely determined that they shall be so handled as to sub serve the public good. We draw the line against misconduct, not against wealth."

"Our duty to the whole, including the unborn generations, bids us to restrain an unprincipled present-day minority from wasting the heritage of these unborn generations. The movement for the conservation of wildlife and the larger movement for the conservation of all our natural resources are essentially democratic in spirit, purpose, and method."

"Our government, National and State, must be freed from the sinister influence or control of special interests. Exactly as the special interests of cotton and slavery threatened our political integrity before the Civil War, so now the great special business interests too often control and corrupt the men and methods of government for their own profit. We must drive the special interests out of politics."

"Patriotism means to stand by the country. It does not mean to stand by the president or any other public official, save exactly to the degree in which he himself stands by the country. It is patriotic to support him insofar as he efficiently serves the country. It is unpatriotic not to oppose him to the exact extent that by inefficiency or otherwise he fails in his duty to stand by the country. In either event, it is unpatriotic not to tell the truth, whether about the president or anyone else."

"People ask the difference between a leader and a boss ... The leader works in the open, and the boss in covert. The leader leads, and the boss drives."

"Politeness [is] a sign of dignity, not subservience."

"Practical equality of opportunity for all citizens, when we achieve it, will have two great results. First, every man will have a fair chance to make of himself all that in him lies; to reach the highest point to which his capacities, unassisted by special privilege of his own and unhampered by the special privilege of others, can carry him, and to get for himself and his family substantially what he has earned. Second, equality of opportunity means that the commonwealth will get from every citizen the highest service of which he is capable. No man who carries the burden of the special privileges of another can give to the commonwealth that service to which it is fairly entitled."

"Right here let me make as vigorous a plea as I know how in favor of saying nothing that we do not mean, and of acting without hesitation up to whatever we say. A good many of you are probably acquainted with the old proverb: 'Speak softly and carry a big stick -- you will go far.' If a man continually blusters, if he lacks civility, a big stick will not save him from trouble; and neither will speaking softly avail, if back of the softness there does not lie strength, power. In private life there are few beings more obnoxious than the man who is always loudly boasting; and if the boaster is not prepared to back up his words his position becomes absolutely contemptible. So it is with the nation. It is both foolish and undignified to indulge in undue self-glorification, and, above all, in loose-tongued denunciation of other peoples."

"So that his place shall never be with those cold and timid souls who knew neither victory nor defeat"

"The absence of effective State, and, especially, national, restraint upon unfair money-getting has tended to create a small class of enormously wealthy and economically powerful men, whose chief object is to hold and increase their power. The prime need to is to change the conditions which enable these men to accumulate power which it is not for the general welfare that they should hold or exercise. We grudge no man a fortune which represents his own power and sagacity, when exercised with entire regard to the welfare of his fellows. Again, comrades over there, take the lesson from your own experience. Not only did you not grudge, but you gloried in the promotion of the great generals who gained their promotion by leading their army to victory. So it is with us. We grudge no man a fortune in civil life if it is honorably obtained and well used. It is not even enough that it should have been gained without doing damage to the community. We should permit it to be gained only so long as the gaining represents benefit to the community."

"The best executive is the one who has sense enough to pick good men to do what he wants done, and self-restraint to keep from meddling with them while they do it."

"The conservation of natural resources is the fundamental problem. Unless we solve that problem it will avail us little to solve all others"

"The credit belongs to the man who is actually in the arena, whose face is marred by dust and sweat and blood, who knows the great enthusiasms, the great devotions, and spends himself in a worthy cause; who at best, if he wins, knows the thrills of high achievement, and, if he fails, at least fails daring greatly, so that his place shall never be with those cold and timid souls who know neither victory or defeat."

"The death-knell of the republic had rung as soon as the active power became lodged in the hands of those who sought, not to do justice to all citizens, rich and poor alike, but to stand for one special class and for its interests as opposed to the interests of others."

"The great body of our citizens shoot less as times goes on. We should encourage rifle practice among schoolboys, and indeed among all classes, as well as in the military services by every means in our power. Thus, and not otherwise, may we be able to assist in preserving peace in the world... The first step – in the direction of preparation to avert war if possible, and to be fit for war if it should come – is to teach men to shoot!"

"The great corporations which we have grown to speak of rather loosely as trusts are the creatures of the State, and the State not only has the right to control them, but it is duty bound to control them wherever the need of such control is shown."

"The greatest gift life has to offer is the opportunity to work hard at work worth doing."

"The joy of living is his who has the heart to demand it."

"The lack of power to take joy in outdoor nature is as real a misfortune as the lack of power to take joy in books"

"The longer I live the more I think of the quality of fortitude... men who fall, pick themselves up and stumble on, fall again, and are trying to get back up when they die."

"The majority in a democracy has no more right to tyrannize over a minority than, under a different system, the latter would to oppress the former."

"The more I see the better satisfied I am that I am an American; free born and free bred, where I acknowledge no man as my superior, except for his own worth, or as my inferior, except for his own demerit."

"The most important single ingredient in the formula of success is knowing how to get along with people."

"The most practical kind of politics is the politics of Decency."

"The nation behaves well if it treats its natural resources as assets which it must turn over to the next generation increased, and not impaired, in value."

"The only man who never makes mistakes is the man who never does anything."

"The President and the Congress are all very well in their way. They can say what they think they think, but it rests with the Supreme Court to decide what they have really thought."

"The reason fat men are good natured is they can neither fight nor run."

"The teachings of the Bible are so interwoven and entwined with our whole civic and social life that it would be literally impossible for us to figure to ourselves what that life would be if these teaching were removed."

"The things that will destroy America are prosperity at any price, peace at any price, safety first instead of duty first and love of soft living and the get-rich-quick theory of life."

"The unforgivable crime is soft hitting. Do not hit at all if it can be avoided, but NEVER hit softly."

"The very pathetic myth of "beneficent nature" could not deceive even the least wise being if he once saw for himself the iron cruelty of life in the tropics. Of course "nature"-- in common parlance a wholly inaccurate term, by the way, especially when used as if to express a single entity--is entirely ruthless, no less so as regards types than as regards individuals, and entirely indifferent to good or evil, and works out her ends or no ends with utter disregard of pain and woe."

"Then there was Micah Jenkins, the Captain of Troop K, a gentle and courteous South Carolinian, on whom danger acted like wine. In action he was a perfect gamecock."

"There are many good people who are denied the supreme blessing of children, and for these we have the respect and sympathy always due to those who, from no fault of their own, are denied any of the other great blessings of life. But the man or woman who deliberately foregoes these blessings, whether from viciousness, coldness, shallow-heartedness, self-indulgence, or mere failure to appreciate aright the difference between the all-important and the unimportant — why, such a creature merits contempt as hearty as any visited upon the soldier who runs away in battle, or upon the man who refuses to work for the support of those dependent upon him, and who though able-bodied is yet content to eat in idleness the bread which others provide."

"There are two things that I want you to make up your minds to: first, that you are going to have a good time as long as you live – I have no use for the sour-faced man – and next, that you are going to do something worthwhile, that you are going to work hard and do the things you set out to do."

"There has never yet been a person in our history who led a life of ease whose name is worth remembering."

"There is not a man of us who does not at times need a helping hand to be stretched out to him, and then shame upon him who will not stretch out the helping hand to his brother."

"There is not one among us in whom a devil does not dwell; at some time, on some point, that devil masters each of us... It is not having been in the Dark House, but having left it, that counts."

"There is quite enough sorrow and shame and suffering and baseness in real life and there is no need for meeting it unnecessarily in fiction. As Police Commissioner it was my duty to deal with all kinds of squalid misery and hideous and unspeakable infamy, and I should have been worse than a coward if I had shrunk from doing what was necessary; but there would have been no use whatever in my reading novels detailing all this misery and squalor and crime, or at least in reading them as a steady thing. Now and then there is a powerful but sad story which really is interesting and which really does good; but normally the books which do good and the books which healthy people find interesting are those which are not in the least of the sugar-candy variety, but which, while portraying foulness and suffering when they must be portrayed, yet have a joyous as well as a noble side."

"There were all kinds of things I was afraid of at first, ranging from grizzly bears to 'mean' horses and gunfighters; but by acting as if I was not afraid I gradually ceased to be afraid."

"This country will not be a good place for any of us to live in unless we make it a good place for all of us to live in."

"To announce that there must be no criticism of the President, or that we are to stand by the President, right or wrong, is not only unpatriotic and servile, but is morally treasonable to the American public."

"To befoul the unholy alliance between corrupt business corrupt politics is the first task of the statesmanship of the day."

"To educate a person in the mind but not in morals is to educate a menace to society."

"To waste, to destroy our natural resources, to skin and exhaust the land instead of using it so as to increase its usefulness, will result in undermining in the days of our children the very prosperity which we ought by right to hand down to them amplified and developed."

"We Americans have many grave problems to solve, many threatening evils to fight, and many deeds to do, if, as we hope and believe, we have the wisdom, the strength, and the courage and the virtue to do them. But we must face facts as they are. We must neither surrender ourselves to a foolish optimism, nor succumb to a timid and ignoble pessimism."

"We are the heirs of the ages"

"We cordially believe in the rights of property. We think that normally and in the long run the rights of humanity, coincide with the rights of property... But we feel that if in exceptional cases there is any conflict between the rights of property and the rights of man, then we must stand for the rights of man."

"We demand that big business give the people a square deal; in return we must insist that when any one engaged in big business honestly endeavors to do right he shall himself be given a square deal."

"We despise and abhor the bully, the brawler, the oppressor, whether in private or public life, but we despise no less the coward and the voluptuary. No man is worth calling a man who will not fight rather than submit to infamy or see those that are dear to him suffer wrong."

"We must beware of any attempt to make hatred in any form the basis of action. Most emphatically each of us needs to stand up for his own rights; all men and all groups of men are bound to retain their self-respect, and, demanding this same respect from others, to see that they are not injured and that they have secured to them the fullest liberty of thought and action. But to feed fat a grudge against others, while it may or may not harm them, is sure in the long run to do infinitely greater harm to the man himself."

"We must hold to a rigid accountability those public servants who show unfaithfulness to the interests of the nation or inability to rise to the high level of the new demands upon our strength and our resources."

"We should not forget that it will be just as important to our descendants to be prosperous in their time as it is to us to be prosperous in our time."

"We want men who will fix their eyes on the stars, but who will not forget that their feet must walk on the ground."

"When they call the roll in the Senate, the Senators do not know whether to answer 'Present' or 'Not Guilty'."

"When you play, play hard; when you work, don't play at all."

"When you're at the end of your rope, tie a knot and hold on"

"Wide differences of opinion in matters of religious, political, and social belief must exist if conscience and intellect alike are not to be stunted, if there is to be room for healthy growth."

"With self discipline most anything is possible."

"Women should have free access to every field of labor which they care to enter, and when their work is as valuable as that of a man it should be paid as highly."

Made in United States
Troutdale, OR
12/19/2023

16150593R00040